Some Kids Use Wheelchairs

Revised and Updated

by Lola M. Schaefer

Consulting Editor: Gail Saunders-Smith, PhD

Consultant: Nancy Dobson, Director
Pediatric Therapy Services, Mankato, Minnesota

Capstone

Mankato, Minnesota

Pebble Books are published by Capstone Press,
151 Good Counsel Drive, P.O. Box 669, Mankato, Minnesota 56002.
www.capstonepress.com

1 2 3 4 5 6 12 11 10 09 08 07

Library of Congress Cataloging-in-Publication Data
Schaefer, Lola M., 1950–
    Some kids use wheelchairs / by Lola M. Schaefer.—Rev. and updated.
    p. cm.—(Pebble books. Understanding differences)
    Includes bibliographical references and index.
    ISBN-13: 978-1-4296-0812-1 (hardcover)
    ISBN-10: 1-4296-0812-9 (hardcover)
    1. Children with disabilities—Transportation—Juvenile literature. 2. Children with
disabilities—Orientation and mobility—Juvenile literature. 3. Wheelchairs—Juvenile
literature. I. Title. II. Series.
HV3022.S33 2008
362.4′30973—dc22   2007009115

Summary: Simple text and photographs discuss why some kids cannot walk, how
    wheelchairs help them, and the everyday activities of children who use wheelchairs.

Note to Parents and Teachers

The Understanding Differences set supports national social studies
standards related to individual development and identity. This
book describes children and illustrates the special needs of children
who use wheelchairs. The photographs support early readers in
understanding the text. The repetition of words and phrases helps
early readers learn new words. This book also introduces early
readers to subject-specific vocabulary words, which are defined in
the Glossary. Early readers may need assistance to read some words
and to use the Table of Contents, Glossary, Read More, Internet
Sites, and Index sections of the book.

Table of Contents

Why Kids Use Wheelchairs

Some kids use wheelchairs. Kids who cannot walk use wheelchairs to go places.

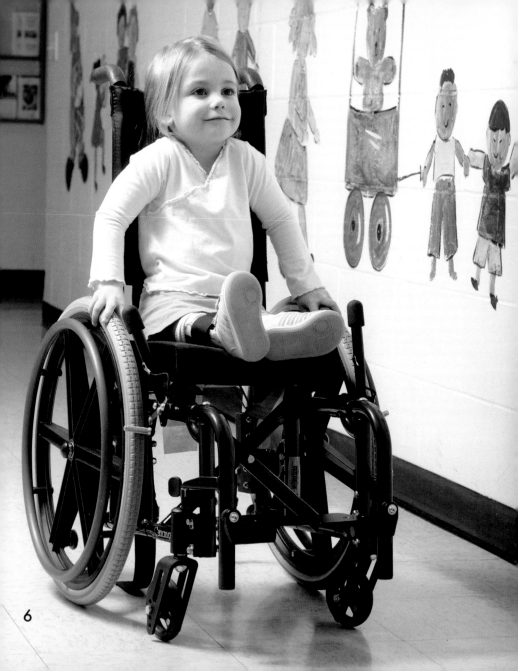

Some kids cannot walk because they were born with weak bones or muscles. Other kids use a wheelchair after they get hurt.

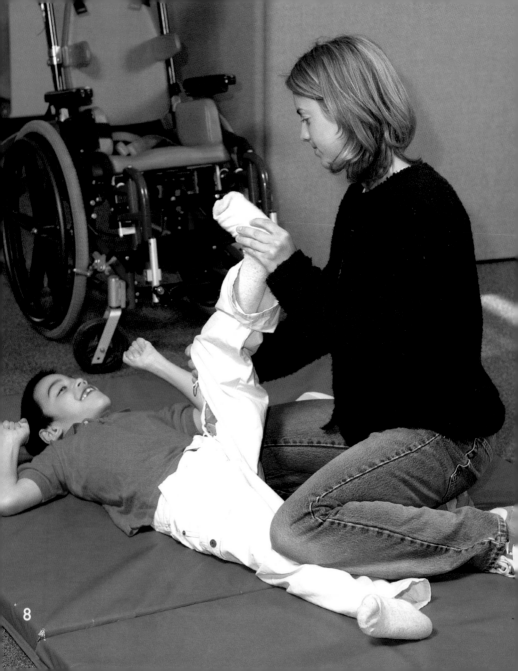

Being Active

Physical therapists help kids who use wheelchairs stretch their muscles.

Some kids who use wheelchairs go swimming. The exercise is good for their muscles.

Everyday Life

Kids who use wheelchairs go many places.
They use ramps to get into vans.

They use ramps to enter and exit buildings.

Kids who use wheelchairs go to the library. They read books and use computers.

Some kids who use wheelchairs play sports. They like to have fun.

Some kids who use
wheelchairs go to camp.
They follow trails
through the woods.

Glossary

physical therapist—a person trained to give treatment to people who are hurt or have physical disabilities; massage and exercise are two kinds of treatment.

ramp—a flat area that slants to connect two levels; ramps allow people in wheelchairs to get into buildings and vans.

wheelchair—a type of chair on wheels for people who are ill, hurt, or have physical disabilities; wheelchairs can be pushed by hand or by motor.

Read More

Dwight, Laura. *Brothers and Sisters.* New York: Star Bright Books, 2005.

Royston, Angela. *Using a Wheelchair.* What's it Like? Chicago: Heinemann Library, 2005.

Schaefer, Adam. *Tools that Help Me.* The World around Me. Vero Beach, Fla,: Rourke, 2007.

Internet Sites

FactHound offers a safe, fun way to find Internet sites related to this book. All of the sites on FactHound have been researched by our staff.

Here's how:

1. Visit *www.facthound.com*
2. Choose your grade level.
3. Type in this book ID **1429608129** for age-appropriate sites. You may also browse subjects by clicking on letters, or by clicking on pictures and words.
4. Click on the **Fetch It** button.

FactHound will fetch the best sites for you!   23

Index

Word Count: 121
Early-Intervention Level: 12

Editorial Credits

Rebecca Glaser, revised edition editor; Mari C. Schuh, editor; Bob Lentz, revised
    edition designer; Katy Kudela, photo researcher; Kelly Garvin, photo stylist

Photo Credits

Capstone Press/Karon Dubke, 6, 12, 14, 16
Getty Images Inc./Taxi, cover
Gregg R. Andersen, 8
Marilyn Moseley LaMantia, 20
Muscular Dystrophy Association, 4, 10, 18

Capstone Press thanks Nancy Dobson and the staff of Pediatric Therapy Services in
Mankato, Minnesota, for their assistance with photographs for this book.